ROGER McGOUGH

ANOTHER CUSTARD PIE

ILLUSTRATED by GRAHAM PERCY

Collins

An Imprint of HarperCollinsPublishers

First published in Great Britain by
HarperCollins Publishers Ltd in 1993
First published in Picture Lions in 1993
Picture Lions is an imprint of the Children's Division,
part of HarperCollins Publishers Limited,
77-85 Fulham Palace Road, Hammersmith, London W6 8JB

A CIP record for this title is available
from the British Library.
ISBN 0 00 193742 1
ISBN 0 00 664351 5

Set in 21/32 Futura Book
Printed and bound in Great Britain
by BPCC Paulton Books

I went to bed and dreamed...

Of running away to join the circus.

In the morning, imagine my surprise to find

That the circus had run away to join ME!

There is a lion in the wardrobe
And it's trying on all my clothes.

There is a seal in the bath
With a potty on its nose.

There is a Big Top in the living-room
With sawdust and a ring

And a ring-master who cracks a whip
That packs a mighty sting.

A conjurer in the corner
Delights with sleight of hand.

A baby elephant plays 'chopsticks'
On the baby grand.

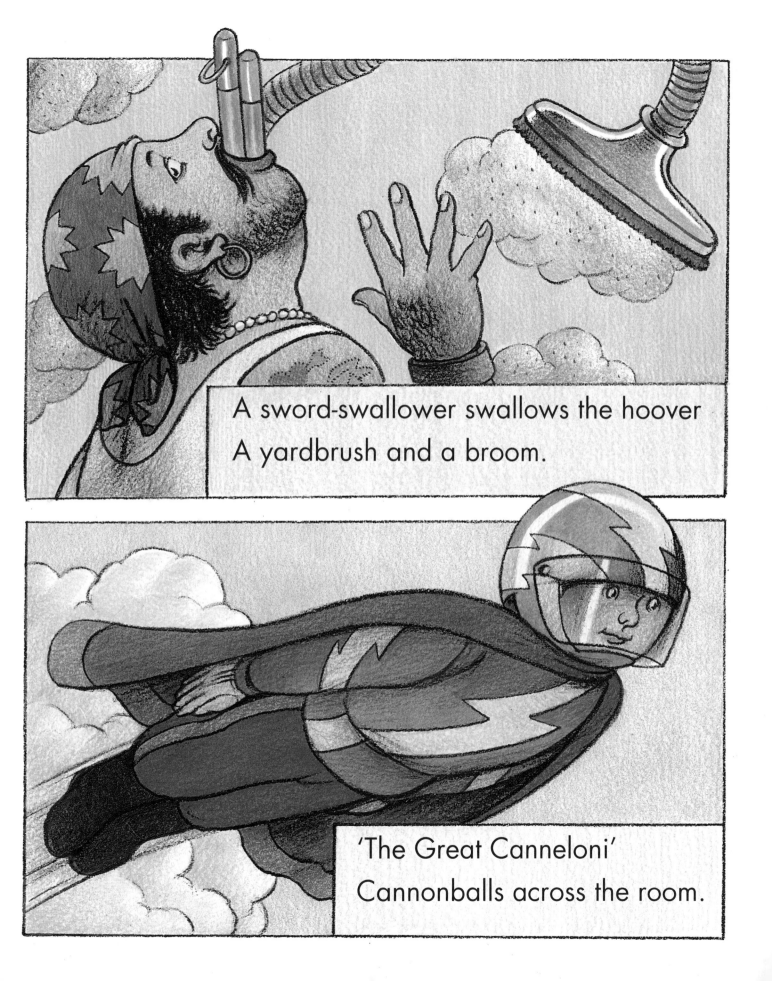

A sword-swallower swallows the hoover
A yardbrush and a broom.

'The Great Canneloni'
Cannonballs across the room.

Baby sister puts her head
Inside a tiger's jaws.

A piper charms a nest of vipers
From a chest of drawers.

In the fireplace, a fire-eater
Eats the flames and licks his lips.

Blindfold on the bannister
A balancer almost slips.

Mum on a galloping pony
Does amazing backward flips.

Dad on a monocycle
Tries to show off, and trips
(He really should be wearing
His monocycle clips).

A monkey on a motorbike
Races round the Wall of Death.

Grandad hides in the aquarium
(And he's getting short of breath).

A lion-tamer, name of Leo,
Teaches Tiddles clever tricks.

A STRONGMAN in the garage
Lifts the car while chewing bricks.

A juggler in the kitchen
Is spinning our best plates,

As Hippo races round him
On a pair of roller-skates.

(While his partner, even bigger,
Does a string of figure eights).

In the toilet, a trapeze artist
Swings as high as he can...

And then, oh dear, disappears
Right into the pan.

On the washing-line in the garden
A tightrope-walker struts.

In the granny flat, a gorilla
Is feeding granny monkey nuts.

A chimpanzee is pouring tea
Out of a chimney pot.

A fakir doing a rope-trick
Ties himself into a knot.

There are clowns in the cloakroom.
If I see another one I'll cry.

Oh, please Mister Clown
Not another custard pie!

A polar bear on a pogo-stick
Is bringing down the plaster.
On the tumble-drier, tumbling twins
Tumble ever faster.

Acrobats in the belfy
Practise somersaults,

While a pair of alligators
Dance the Skater's Waltz.

An Indian Chief (from Basingstoke)
How cheerfully he talks...

As he pins Aunt Flo against the door
With blazing tomahawks.

The house is in a shambles
I can't read or watch T.V.
The polar bear's been at the fridge
There's nothing left for tea.
(Except for custard pies, of course,
But already I've had three).

How I hate the smell of greasepaint
And this crazy jamboree.

Oh I do wish that the circus
Would run away from me.